I0876017

Odette Alonso was born in Santiago de Cuba and has lived in Mexico since 1992. In addition to a novel and two volumes of short stories, she has published twenty poetry collections, receiving numerous prizes, including the 1999 Nicolás Guillén International Poetry Prize and the 2019 Clemencia Isaura Poetry Prize. She won the 2017 Zacatecas National Poetry Prize for *Old Music Island*. Odette served as editor for *Antología de la poesía cubana del exilio* (2011) and co-edited the anthology *Versas y Diversas* (2020), a collection of contemporary lesbian poetry from Mexico. She is currently coordinator for the Bulevar Arcoíris, a cultural project that promotes gender-dissident art and literature. Her most recent publication is *De humo y miel: 35 años de poesía* (2024).

Liz Rose lives and writes on the occupied ancestral lands of the Tohono O'odham Nation and the Pascua Yaqui Tribe. They translate from Spanish and Portuguese and research the intersections of queer and trans theory and Black feminist theory in contemporary lyric writing, performance, and oral histories across the Americas. Liz's broader scholarly and artistic investments include public-facing projects related to translation and reparative archival practices. Their translation of Iliana Rosabal's poetry collection *Fifth Necessity* was published by Wayne State College Press in 2025, and their recent critical work has appeared or is forthcoming in *Siren!*, *College Literature*, and *Trans Studies Quarterly*.

THE PRIDE LIST

EDITED BY BISHAN SAMADDAR

The Pride List presents works of queer literature to the world. An eclectic collection of books of queer stories, poems, plays, biographies, histories, thoughts, ideas, experiences and explorations, the Pride List does not focus on any specific region, nor on any specific genre, but celebrates the great diversity of LGBTQ+ lives across countries, languages, centuries and identities, with the conviction that queer pride comes from its unabashed expression.

OTHER POETRY TITLES IN **THE PRIDE LIST**

KO-HUA CHEN
Decapitated Poetry
Translated from the Chinese by
Wen-chi Li and Colin Bramwell

KIM HYUN
Glory Hole
Translated from the Korean by
Suhyun J. Ahn and Archana Madhavan

CYRIL WONG
Beachlight

CYRIL WONG
Infinity Diary

OLD MUSIC ISLAND

ODETTE ALONSO

Translated from the Spanish by

LIZ ROSE

LONDON NEW YORK CALCUTTA

Seagull Books, 2026

Originally published in Spanish, 2017

First published in English translation by Seagull Books, 2026

Cover design: Sunandini Banerjee, Seagull Books

ISBN 978 1 80309 670 4

British Library Cataloguing-in-Publication Data

A catalogue record for this book is available from the British Library

Typeset by Seagull Books, Calcutta, India

Contents

There exists in the midst of time
the possibility of an island.

MICHEL HOUELLEBECQ

Binding this Nonsense to a finer Knot
Casting to the Winds all common Care
Like a Bell that throws its Nature to the Air.

DJUNA BARNES

You can read this poetry collection while listening to the playlist that inspired it:

Portico

Birds emerging from your mouth
fill the day with reverberations.
The light they leave
tangles between threads of the distaff
erupting in a transparent tapestry.
Song flows out
as you open your chest
and rest against the wall.
I
sitting at your feet
dream all of it.

THE DANCE

A woman dances in my ears

CRISTINA PERI ROSSI

The Proposal

That night
your eyes were the ones that talked
they jumped over silt and swamps
over fecund earth
and desert
over asphalt animals.
Dance with me
you proposed.
Let us be the secret
the centuries we carry on our backs
this music box
and the dance calling.
Let us be the wind and the sea
the hours of our invention.

The Invitation

The message you wrote on paper
is a covert invitation.
Everyone saw the numbers
the phrases
repeated them like gibberish.
Only you and I knew
the true language they hid
the blade of your fingernails
the promise.

The Beginning

It's not so strange to be here
after all.
We danced one night
our reflection in that mirror
our bodies two embers
two violet clouds.
The waltz rocked us
our waists bound together.
Corner smiles remained glowing
and a smell of jasmine
nighttime suitor.

The Fear

That thread
is pulling old songs
a dream of pins
from my mouth.
We were a rumor of fabric
and lavender
a luck of cloudscape.
We smoked menthols
and I wore my grandfather's jacket
and his cologne.
Halfhearted laughter
transforms into a grimace
but squeezing your hand
dispels the fear.

The Desire

The moment I see you
my eye detaches from its socket
suspended from nothingness
travels
in aqueous afternoon gaze
and it's your hands
that return the world to its heartbeat
and desire to this inevitable point
where it again explodes.

The Scent

A particle
the birth of a scent
an invisible finger caressing
igniting
testing the desolate
landscape
long since terrifying.
An interstice
mint and tobacco
mouth ajar.

The Orchestra

We preferred the blues
that your steps keep time
with that box of gratuitous
illusions.
The flight of your skirt
a time of insomnia
along the acetate railing
the time of the tambourine
of bass and brass.
Our time.

The Ballroom

Clove on skin
almond-scented
sweeping dance halls
where marble is a glimmer of another time.
La orquesta tropical
and the big band
blare
like midsummer courtyards
humming inside the body
glued to my body
dancing.

The Public

The railing is not tall enough
to keep us from the gaze of passersby
as they climb the steep
little street.
They take the child by the hand
and when they lift their gaze
discover us
two silhouettes drawn across glass
covered with an inexplicable light.
The child's finger signals.
The moon shines through the clouds.

The Music

On cork the heat
and on wood
the drawing embroiders a name.
The name a riddle
attenuated light beside the piano
that cadence.
The needle falls again on the record
and your neck
dazzling white
dances.
Dressed in a light robe
you purify the aura
and the gaze.

The Rehearsal

We dance.
My tongue paints planets on your skin.
My hands cannot stop at your waist.
You smell of honey
of the latest compact powder.
Your shoulder fruit flesh
where I sink teeth
my saliva a rushing river in your mouth.
Your body's warmth is a wager.
All eyes watching the dance
disappear
when I brush against your lips.

The Dance

The doors are closed
and we are on this liquid bed.
My eyes invent your skin
delineate the curve of your back
the sensual delight of your chest
the fuss of hands.
Your lips
learn the language they speak
caressing
painting a dissected heart.
Feet trace figures in the air
and we create that distant land of ours.
Desire doesn't end
it traverses us
and love
is this dance we weave.

GEMINI DAYS

I just wanted you to see my heart!

SOR JUANA INÉS DE LA CRUZ

For love there is no heaven, love, only this day.

ROSARIO CASTELLANOS

Desires

For Paulina

I seek but three desires
a drink at the day's edge
a mirror in which to laugh
unhurried
and the yes hidden in words
I still don't say.
But three desires
the sea and its scent
measured rhythm of the mare
night fragment that never was.
Time
this flutter amidst shadows
finger on lips in a sign of silence
smoke and scar.
Three desires I crave.
I want the first stitch of fabric
the scream of your eyes watching me
and all the time
thereafter.

A Version of Things

Soared the lock
saw the path.
A bird ascended above the sea
slipstream left in the wake of her hand.
She went to Tokyo
or Egypt
or to the hollow of other hands
that woman of absurd eyes
distorted voice.

You make the bed you lie in
alone
in drawn-out night
and the night
which is all you have
shelters you.

What would happen if those air kisses
were now in that specific mouth
through which to swirl
the gilded sustenance of drink.

Her mouth
the idea of her mouth
left for Tokyo
or Egypt
or for the dream of other mouths.

Animal of obscure lineage.
Grief.

Zero Point

Out of the corner of my eye an arrow targets me
your perfume gives folly to the afternoon.
The kiss hangs like insect flight
from an invisible thread
drawn through the air.
Could it be called a kiss
that spark
distant from biting lips
from ardor evoked in that word.
Time passes
across the immutable
two.

This is the zero point
of love.

Voodoo

She placed a handmade box
with a floral motif
into the palm of my hand.
Inside
four voodoo pins
four small children
nailed to my body.
That would be yours
she said
even if I had to shove
an arrow between the legs
into that viscera called the heart.
Prophetic butterflies flew by
a flutter heard
and in the shadows
the click of a
nonexistent tongue.

Woman of Water

That woman has a cat on her shoulder
and a name that tears at skin
skin that refuses the word
appeals to friction
to the voiceless utterance.
That woman questions me with her onerous eyes
traces pathways to the land
where water baptizes.
The wound bleeds
perhaps the knee
perhaps in that unspeakable place
and the water cries the name
yearning.
That woman waits
and I long to reach her.

Trepidation

Do not call passion by name
call it friendship
misfortune
inexplicable coincidence.
Do not say *corazón*
or *beso*
or *fortuna*
but kiss her lips
and strip your words of trepidation.

Stones

I am
in each one of those stones.
The waters of my body
bathe you now
each breath flies away with time
to name things we did not yet know.
In each of those stones
I rest my hand
as if it were drawing
star maps
wisps of smoke
on your skin.
On each one
I place a kiss
that you might feel it.

Memory Games

Between my fingers
woolen tresses
dewy
on the brink of the afternoon
becoming
lubricous.
My tongue
brackish
begins an eternity on your chest.
Behind the curtains
a silent scream
your fingernails in my back.
All dreams converge in the moment
of eruption.
Our eyes have preserved the memory.

Phosphorous

Neither the circle we made with our hands
nor breath of prescient mouth
was enough for the small
almost innocuous flame.
It torched everything around.
A conflagration.

Venom

The venom has been inoculated
a couple of drops were enough.
You can try to flee
run the rest of the night
the rest of your life
and you will not have moved from that place.
My tongue will continue whispering
words you do not want to hear
and there will be no salvation or forgetting.
It's too late.

Shameless

The threshold
and a staircase.
Descend.
Take from your hands
the wave covering us
waters where we see each other
like mirrors
eyes blurry
cubist smile
shameless women.

Agave Nectar

What I want is that other honey
sticky between fingers
and I suck
hungry.
Sweet of taste
and fragrance.
That other
ultimate honey
joins the lip
and spreads
addiction
with a surrendering acidity.

Box of Mirrors

In that box of mirrors
there is no glass that does not reflect
the intensity of light
its temporal absence
the heat emanating
from embracing bodies
trembling
as if all magic
will begin
and end
between their mouths.

Azul

Blue
your legs resemble the night
they navigate a swarm
of alcohol
and desire.
Smoking
your mouth would seem to whisper a sentence
a verse
bilabial
and final.
I touch your legs
and my eyes squint
in the stagnant air of the bar.
My firm hand
is our fate.
There is no word to name you.
Only *el azul.*

Noche de San Juan

We scatter paper ashes
over the earth
annotations of our desire
a thread barely visible
spider web
swaying golden lightness
with winged harmony.
Words are diluted
beneath that tree
and everything I did
accumulates like dust
in the cracks.

Artifice

In the train
that intimate episode
wanted to be flesh.
How many nights
upon arriving at the station
I saw your mouth
how many times I wanted to prolong that second
with a kiss that wasn't rejected
how many hours later
in the semidarkness
I said your name.

The sun drops leaden
noises undampened
the scent
sweat of time down my armpits
drowning forehead.
Inside
the afternoon unfolds into our time
Friday a bubble
this balcony
you and me.

Dance upon my body
cloudspirit.
Mark directions on the map
according to your taste
and take what you desire
water
elixirs
the unending smile.
Leave me that artifice
poetry.

Gemini Days

I will come for you
at the time of the waters
Gemini days
of flaming torches.
I will come for you
and the earth will be
a coffer where I sow your gaze.
Do you remember that night of glass
of steam in the window?
Thus we will be
shadow theater
the trace of a desire.
I will come for you
the heat will come relenting in the current
in the warm herb aroma
and there will be a color
perhaps blue
with which to name you.

Voyeur

You saw a door ajar
and two shadows
heads drawing near.
But you did not see her lips on mine
nor her elusive gaze
nor did you hear my mouth whisper to her
nor see the gesture with which we said goodbye.

Rainy Season

Now that it's raining
and time is no longer enough
I think of your legs
open for me
that afternoon when everything was bodies
your sap spilling into my mouth
the sweet bite
that trembling returning each night
when I say your name.

Despeinada

In the first car
wind
tousles you
and the scent of your hair
reaches the fifth car
where I relive
the moment
of your scent.
Amber
lightning strikes the air
its stealthy flight
separates us
but wherever you go
the line
the monosyllable
an infinity of silent verbs
will follow.

Mind Map

I know the scene
I can see you busying about the kitchen
inventing the paradise of dinner
searching the screen for dressing.
I imagine the path of your steps
the corner where you would sit craving my kisses.
I know the window
where you dance for me
and I enter the room
imagining what you do
once you close the door.

The Last Shot

The red light at the end of the shot
indicated proximity
airport corridors
sleepless mornings
sunrises.
I dreamed I kissed you
and in a moment we were alone again.
We built a false landscape
our backs to the return ring.
Cold bed
cold trunk of tricks
only darkness waits
faithful
in the corners.

And Sail Away

Forgetting is diluted in this dialogue of gestures.
Your dress
that afternoon I wasn't there
the tide
spreading such morbid sand
over your body.
The sea carries a blessing
there are footprints that persist
in that fertile earth of silence
and forgetfulness sinks between luminescence
rising of celebrations on skin
a dance that was mine
and you refused me.
There are dreams that should not be cast to the wind
nor into doubt.
Let us sail away together.
On this ship
there is neither wreckage
nor oblivion.

Old Music Island

All music is yesterday.
The zither song precedes us
permeates walls
in the middle of nowhere.
All music
is a game of illusions
an ancient currency
spinning
through the interweave of our experience.
Come evening
there will be
reverberations
chasms
a flight of birds
emerging from your mouth
carry us
to that island of smoke
and music.

TRANSLATOR'S ACKNOWLEDGMENTS

The following poems included in the manuscript were previously published in journals and print anthologies:

Odette Alonso, "Pórtico / Portico," in *Annuario de poesia de San Diego / San Diego Poetry Annual* (San Diego, CA: Garden Oak Press, 2021).

Odette Alonso, "The Proposal," *Volume*, no. 1 (2020).